hindi
KAY BOL

Yayyyy! It's Monday!
फिर आया सोमवार

यह किताब......................की है।

This book belongs to ....

लेखन — प्रिया गुप्ता
चित्रांकन — मेघांश

This book is for my children, for they find joy in simple things. Also, I would like to thank every trash worker in the world.

यह किताब मेरे बच्चों के लिए है, क्योंकि वे साधारण में भी खुशी ढूँढ लेते हैं। हर कूड़ा कर्मी को मेरा धन्यवाद!

••• Priya...!

Copyright © Priya Gupta, 2023

www.hindikaybol.com

All Rights Reserved.

Designed by 'www.arcreativewings.com'

No part of this publication may be reproduced, distributed, or transmitted in any form or by any means, including photocopying, recording, or other electronic or mechanical methods, without the prior written permission of the author, except in the case of brief quotations embodied in critical reviews and certain other non-commercial uses permitted by copyright law.

www.hindikaybol.com
Follow us on FB / IG @ hindikaybol

ISBN Hindi Edition: 978-93-5426-433-7

ISBN Hindi-English Paperback: 978-93-5895-932-1

ISBN Hindi-English Hardcover: 978-93-5891-589-1

It's a Monday! There's something special today.

आज सोमवार है। आज कुछ ख़ास है!

We wake up at 7 o'clock every day. Today, my brother and I got up at 6 o'clock. Do you want to know why?

रोज़ हम सात बजे उठते हैं।
आज मैं और मेरा भाई छः बजे उठ गए।
पूछिए क्यों?

What made us get up so early?
Mom is quite amused.

फिर हम क्यों जल्दी उठे?
माँ भी हैरान है।

करे

We looked at the clock once more.
And then we heard it coming- "Vroooooooom!" Off we ran!

हमने एक और बार घड़ी की तरफ़ देखा।
आगे सड़क से आवाज़ आई - व्रोउम्म्म्म! हम भागे।

We opened the window and sat wide-eyed.
We could see it far away.
Big, yellow, and strong – the trash pick-up truck.

हमने खिड़की खोली और ताक लगाकर बैठ गए।
वह दूर से आता दिख रहा था। बड़ा, पीला, और ताकतवर-हमारा कूड़े का ट्रक!

It stopped right outside our house.
Its big arm came forward and emptied the trash can in its belly.

वह घर के बाहर रूका, उसका हाथ आगे आया,
और उसने हमारे कूड़ेदान को अपने अन्दर पलट लिया।

We were thrilled. The truck driver waved at us.

हम बहुत खुश हुए। फिर ट्रक ड्राइवर ने हमें बाय किया।

मेरा भाई सोचता है कि ट्रक सारा कूड़ा खा लेता है!! लेकिन मुझे पता है कि वह कूड़ा कहाँ जाता है।

My brother thinks that the truck gobbles up the trash. But I know better where the trash ends up.

Landfill, where the trash decomposes under the earth.

Recycling plant, where the contents are processed into new things.

हरे कूड़ेदान का कूड़ा लैन्डफिल में जाता है, यानि धरती में दबाया जाता है।
नीले कूड़ेदान का कूड़ा रीसाइकल, यानि फिर से उपयोग किया जाता है।

कूड़ा कम से कम करें। धरती को साफ रखें!
जैसे हम अपने घर को रखते हैं।

Create lesser waste. Keep the earth clean.
Just like we keep our home!

Sort the

प्लास्टिक कप
Plastic cup

खाली गत्ता
Packaging box

कूड़ा

मोटी प्लास्टिक
Thick plastic bottles

अख़बार
Newspaper

trash!

छाटें!

काँच की बोतल
Glass bottle

मैटल कैन
Soda can

दूध की खाली बोतल
Empty milk can

केले का छिलका
Banana peel

Key to difficult words

सोमवार	Monday		आवाज़	Sound
ख़ास	Special		खिड़की	Window
रोज़	Everyday		ताक	Gaze
उठ	Get up / Wake up		ताकतवर	Strong
पूछिए	Ask		कूड़े का ट्रक	Trash truck
बरफ़	Snow		कूड़ेदान	Trash can
जल्दी	Early / Quick		कि	That
हैरान	Surprised		उपयोग	Use
घड़ी	Clock		साफ़	Clean
सड़क	Road		धरती	Earth

Hindi special letters

Some half letters combine with the next consonant and change shape.

Half ट+र = ट्र (tr) as in ट्रक

Half ड+र = ड्र (dr) as in ड्राइवर

Other half letters with र

Half प+र = प्र (pr)

Half क+र = क्र (kr)

Half द+र = द्र (dr)

Half ग+र = ग्र (gr)

Did you know?
English has borrowed many words from Hindi including guru, pyjama, bungalow, jungle, thug etc.

Vowels / स्वर (swar)

अ	आ	इ	ई	उ	ऊ	ऋ
a	aa	i	ee	u	oo	ri

ए	ऐ	ओ	औ	अं	अः	
a	ae	o	au	am	ah	

Consonant / व्यंजन (vyanjan)

क	ख	ग	घ	ङ
ka	kha	ga	gh	ng
च	छ	ज	झ	ञ
ca	cha	ja	jha	ña
ट	ठ	ड	ढ	ण
ṭa	ṭha	ḍa	ḍha	ṇa
त	थ	द	ध	न
ta	tha	da	dha	na
प	फ	ब	भ	म
pa	pha	ba	bha	ma

य	र	ल	व
ya	ra	la	va

श	ष	स	ह
śa	ṣa	sa	ha

क्ष	त्र	ज्ञ
ksh	tra	gya